MW01537631

This book belongs to:

____

Made in the USA
Las Vegas, NV
11 December 2023

82573311R00066